Succeeding at Interviews

*Give great answers and
ask the right questions*

Third edition

Judith Verity

Published by How To Books Ltd,
3 Newtec Place, Magdalen Road,
Oxford OX4 1RE. United Kingdom.
Tel: (01865) 793806. Fax: (01865) 248780
email: info@howtobooks.co.uk
http://www.howtobooks.co.uk

First edition 1999
Second edition 2002
Third edition 2004
Reprinted 2005

British Library Cataloguing in Publication Data.
A catalogue record for this book is available from the British Library.

Produced for How To Books by Deer Park Productions, Tavistock
Typeset by PDQ Typesetting, Newcastle-under-Lyme, Staffordshire
Cover design by Baseline Arts Ltd, Oxford
Printed and bound in Great Britain by Cromwell Press Ltd, Trowbridge,
Wiltshire.

NOTE: The material contained in this book is set out in good faith for general
guidance and no liability can be accepted for loss or expense incurred as a
result of relying in particular circumstances on statements made in this book.
Laws and regulations are complex and liable to change, and readers should
check the current position with the relevant authorities before making
personal arrangements.

Contents

5 Being Remembered for the Right Reasons   **76**

6 Standard Interview Questions   **91**

Preface

*'Everyone sees what you appear to be: few experience what
you really are.'*   *Machiavelli*

*'Well, I got the interview – there's nothing else I can do
except turn up.'*

I've heard comments like that so many times from
candidates who put hours of effort into tailoring their
CV, filling in application forms and writing elegant
letters, only to freeze in interview. Why do they do that?
Because the prejudices of the interviewer will determine
the outcome anyway? Because it will all depend on how
the interviewer and the candidate 'feel' on the day?
Because they may be lucky enough to get the 'right'
questions or unlucky enough to get the 'wrong' ones?

If you spend the days or weeks between application and
interview in limbo (as many candidates do), all this is
probably true. But you have a choice. You can spend that
time profitably in preparing yourself to:

◆ Tune into the interviewer so that you quickly pick up
   what kind of impression he or she wants you to
   make.

- ◆ Make sure that you are in the best possible frame of mind to think quickly and make the most of all the cues you may be offered.

- ◆ Put your interviewer into a receptive, positive state.

- ◆ Practise the standard interview questions so that you don't get caught out by any of them.

Being the best you can be in three-quarters of an hour isn't easy but it doesn't depend on luck. It depends on planning and practice.

As Machiavelli said, if you leave it to chance, you may not do yourself justice. So don't leave anything to chance.

Judith Verity

Chapter 1

Preparing for the Interview

'It doesn't take talent to be on time.'
Pete Reiser, Baseball player

In this Chapter:
- **checking the job out carefully**
- **researching the company**
- **tailoring your CV**
- **setting up a practice group**
- **rehearsing.**

The first thing your interviewer will know about you is whether you turn up, on time, with everything you need. This doesn't take talent or experience, just meticulous preparation, to get comfortably to the point where you give yourself a chance to shine when the moment comes.

In the interview room, you have two tasks: first, to fit your abilities to the needs of the employer and second, to tune in to the interviewer. To do both competently in 30 or 40 minutes and drink coffee at the same time takes preparation and practice. If you want to be ready, on the starting blocks, before the interviewer asks the first question, you need to work on that interview as soon as you put down the phone from making the appointment.

Is this you?

◆ Do you find yourself repeatedly in the wrong job?

◆ Do the positions you really want always seem to go to somebody else?

◆ Despite your best efforts, do you always lose your way to the interview, or turn up without your CV or references?

◆ Do you find yourself stressed and cluttered on arrival, when other candidates look sleek and well organised?

◆ Do questions sometimes take you by surprise?

◆ Do you wish you had some 'inside' knowledge that would help you prepare more adequately?

Checking the job out carefully

Make sure you know enough about the job to be sure it's right for you. Interview skills are so definable and easy to learn that, when you've acquired them, you will need to be more **selective** about your job applications. There's a theory that no interview is wasted because it's a chance to practise your interview skills. But an unsuccessful interview for the right job will lower your morale and waste everybody's time in the short term. And a successful interview for the wrong job will lower your morale and waste everybody's time in the long term.

Health Warning: there are dangers in randomly becoming an expert interviewee. These are powerful skills and, once acquired, should be used with caution – like the three wishes from the magic lamp. Ending up in the wrong job just because you were brilliant in interview isn't going to bring you lasting peace and happiness. And don't rely on the interviewer to weed out the inappropriate applicants – most interviewers are there simply because they have reached senior positions, not because they know how to pick competent recruits.

'The three most important questions all winners ask themselves: What do I want? How am I going to get it? When am I going to do something about it?' Mark Gibson.

Do you know enough to convince the interviewer you're the person they need?

◆ Ask for company information at the same time as you ask for your interview forms.

◆ Search for details on the Internet or in the finance sections of the daily papers.

◆ Look for details, not just on profit and loss, but also about company culture.

◆ Talk to others who have been employed or interviewed by the organisation.

◆ Check that company values are congruent with your own.

◆ Find out the company's policy on employee leave and benefits.

◆ Make sure you know why this particular post is vacant.

Researching the company

Are you one of the relatively small proportion of job seekers who actually bother to find out about the company they are applying to join? Or are you among the majority of applicants who assume there will be plenty of time to check out the pension arrangements once they get the job?

It's well worthwhile taking the time to check out a potential employer in advance. You may be wasting a couple of hours on research if you get turned down at the interview – but what if your research tells you in advance that it's definitely not the job for you? That's a couple of hours you won't have to spend travelling to and from the interview and getting stressed and anxious in between. And it may even save you weeks and months of job dissatisfaction if your superior interview skills land you in a job you aren't going to enjoy.

Why: Two good reasons for researching your potential employers

A good understanding of the company you're applying to join puts you in a stronger position at every stage of the process.

It gives you several advantages in the interview:

◆ It makes you look well organised and well informed.

◆ It saves time. Interviewees usually get only a small proportion of the interview time to ask their own questions. You will look less pushy and you won't waste precious time asking irrelevant questions.

◆ It makes it easier for you to answer the interviewer's questions because you know what sort of person they are looking for and you can tailor your answers accordingly.

◆ If you can show that you understand the product and the company mission, your interviewer may assume you'll need shorter induction training. Anything about you that might save the company money will give you an advantage.

It gives you a flying start on the job. If you're offered the job and you decide to take it, your learning curve will be much shorter. You'll already have a feel for the type of organisation you're joining. You'll fit in faster and find your feet more easily and your job satisfaction levels are likely to rise more rapidly.

Company Information	
Company name Address and other contact details Position applied for Contact person	
Job title Description Main responsibilities Place in the chain of command Salary range Other benefits (pension, health insurance, discounts etc) Hours Holidays	
Interview details Date, time and type of interview	Check on the interview procedure. Will there be more than one interview? Who will interview you? Will there be any psychometric tests? In tray tests? Do they need you to bring anything to the interview? Will there be a job trial (this is usual with jobs which have a practical element to them – chefs for example)?

Company style Size of business Office locations Number of employees at each office Employee benefits	You need to know whether this is the kind of environment that suits you. Do you want to join an organisation that might offer you the chance to work in different locations? Do you prefer smaller or larger offices? What would it be like to work there?
Company details What does it sell? How long has it been in business? What is its market share? What is the turnover? Who owns it? Who are its leading competitors? What are the recent trends in this kind of business? Where does this particular organisation seem to be going? Have there been any scandals or adverse publicity regarding this company?	Can you relate to the product? Is it a stable business that's going to be around for long enough to provide you with promotion opportunities and a pension (if that's what you want)? Some companies offer share options to employees, and, if that's the case, you'll need to know just how valuable those shares are likely to be. Is it ethical (if that's important to you)?

What: Knowing what you want to know

Before you start to research your target organisation, decide what it is that you want to know. It's a good idea to draw up a form or checklist so you can be sure you haven't missed anything. See examples on pages 6–7.

It always surprises me that people often go into an interview – and even accept a job offer – without answers to many of these questions. If you've done that in the past, and maybe regretted it later, you can be much better organised in the future.

How: Doing your detective work

When you've drawn up your checklist, you will probably have a much clearer idea of *what* you need to know about your prospective employers and *why* you need to know it.

The next big question is how to go about getting the information.

The Internet

If you have access to the Internet it's definitely the best way to get information. If you don't have a computer yourself, you can still do your research online.

◆ Ask a friend for help – most people know somebody who's a surfer.

◆ Go to an Internet café – some of them will give you help and advice.

◆ Visit the local library – most of them now have
terminals you can use and the librarians will show
you how to use them. The library may even subscribe
to specialist business research companies like Dun &
Bradstreet or, more likely, to the UK government's
own Companies House.

Once you're online and you start to find your way
around, you'll be amazed at how much information is
available to you, but you can get started straight away
with these suggestions.

◆ **Visit Companies House**
The Companies House website
(*www.companieshouse.gov.uk*) will give you some basic
information for free. If you want more detail,
including copies of accounts, you will have to pay for
it, or subscribe to their fuller service.

◆ **Check out the company directly**
Enter the company name on one of the search
engines (Google is very good) and it will pull up a
list of all the websites which mention that name.
Some will be relevant and some won't, but you'll
soon see which is which.

First check the company's own website. If your target
doesn't have one, that in itself is probably a bad sign
– nowadays almost everybody, regardless of size, has
one. In fact, you can learn quite a lot from the style
and sophistication of the corporate website. Of

course, it will put the most favourable spin on its operations, but the basic facts about office locations, numbers of employees, products, mission and share values will be there. Some companies even have a section on their website which is specifically geared to provide information to prospective employees.

Next, check for any other information about the company that may be available (this is where you're likely to find out the downside, if there is one). In the case of public companies, a Google search for the name will often turn up analysts' reports on financial websites which give some more independent information.

◆ **Check the government websites**
If your prospective employer is a school, hospital or a government organisation, you can use the web to get information on those as well, starting with the government's own statistics:
www.statistics.gov.uk
www.statsbase.gov.uk
www.homeoffice.gov.uk

◆ **Ask Auntie**
The BBC website is a great source of information about all sorts of things from schools and hospitals to local government. The best thing to do is call up *www.news.bbc.co.uk* and take it from there. If, for example, you wanted to know about schools you could check *www.news.bbc.co.uk/hi/english/education/league_tables/default.stm*

◆ **Find out about your new neighbourhood**
If your job search involves relocating, you might also want to find out some more details about where you're going to live. If you enter the name of the place in a search engine you will find many areas have local websites that give you a good feel for what it would be like to live there. But, if you want the facts and figures, take a look at *www.neighbourhood.statistics.gov.uk*

Visit the library

If you really don't want to go online, you could visit the library anyway. Central libraries in particular carry a lot of reports and statistical information about companies and businesses and neighbourhoods. They vary a lot, so call in and ask.

Call the company direct

Sometimes the obvious route is the easiest. Either ask at the time of arranging the interview for company information to be sent out to you, or call separately, ask for the press department and request annual reports and anything else they are currently putting out. If it's a publicly listed company, you have a right to ask for the information – and you can say you're thinking of buying some shares.

Read the press

It's surprising how much you can learn from watching

TV and reading the papers. Once you know you're getting interested in a particular company you'll find its name jumps out at you when you would never have noticed it before.

◆ If you're looking for work with one of the big global conglomerates, or even a small but dynamic publicly listed company, get in the habit of buying the *Financial Times* or reading the city pages of your regular newspaper for a few weeks.

◆ If the company advertises, look at the style and extent of their advertising campaign.

Ask the employees

The best way to find out whether you really want to work in a particular place or not is to talk to people who work there. If you know someone who knows someone who does, then ask for an introduction. Or you could take to hanging out in the winebar nearest the office in the early evening, particularly on a Friday.

Tailoring your CV

Unless there's only one perfect job for you in the world, which is very unlikely, there's no harm in fine tuning your CV to each application. In order to do this, you need to find out as exactly as you can what will be required in interview.

It's as important to know about the method of interviewing as it is about the likely content and focus. For example, if it's a **criteria based** interview, you can ask for the criteria in advance. All this means is that the interview will be **focused** on **requirements of the job** rather than on the interviewee as a whole person and there's a lot more information about this in Chapter 2.

After re-reading and, if possible, discussing with the prospective employer, the job you're applying for, write down a detailed, point by point, job description and then add the personal specification which you think will be required, also point by point. You may be surprised at how much more information you have than you might have thought. For example:

Zoo Keeper Required for lions and tigers. Must have experience. This may be the only information given. You may have been a Zoo Keeper before and think you know all there is to know about the post. But, take the time to write it out as follows:

Job Description
Cleaning out cages of large cats.

Feeding large cats.

Person Specification
Hard worker, able to cope with messy, possibly dangerous job.

Knowledge of very specific dietary requirements and ability to handle raw meat.

Ensuring that large cats are healthy (they are harder and more expensive to replace than their keepers).	Some expert knowledge and keen powers of observation.
Ensuring that cages are secure and the public is safe.	Attention to detail and powers of observation.
Ensuring that the public is well informed. Without the paying public there is no zoo and no job.	Likes people, and animals, ability to communicate.
Ensuring that zoo management and fellow keepers are well informed.	Knowledge of hierarchy and ability to communicate. Needs to be a team player.

When a job, even with scant detail, is broken down in this way, it's easy to see how a CV might be laid out, with past experience appropriately highlighted. The zoo keeper job obviously wouldn't suit a timid vegetarian, however fond of animals they might be, and previous experience would clearly be highly important. Any applicant who liked animals but couldn't communicate with other people would be a non-starter.

'The hardest thing to learn in life is which bridge to cross and which to burn.' David Russell.

When preparing your CV, bear in mind the following points.

♦ Many large companies feed CVs into **scanners** and do a **key word search**. You need to **know in advance** what they are looking for, otherwise you may not even get called to interview. Ask before submitting your CV whether it will be computer scanned. If they won't tell you, it probably is. That is your cue to get more information before you fine-tune the wording.

♦ **Tailoring your CV** also enables you to keep it **succinct** and **readable**. Multi-purpose CVs tend to be over-long, especially when the applicant has many years of work experience. Even CVs that aren't computer scanned will probably be reviewed first time around by an HR executive rather than someone from the department you're applying to. Make sure that your **key points** won't be overlooked.

♦ Leave no gaps in your CV. If there are gaps, you may need to make the dates a little more vague. Employers usually assume that a **hiatus** means **imprisonment**, **mental illness** or **undeclared pregnancies**. If there's a gap with a good reason, like working for VSO in a job related area, then declare it.

♦ Most employers nowadays are **sceptical** of family business involvement and of freelance and consultancy or voluntary work. They will assume that this is a **cover** for **unemployment** unless you can prove that you really were running your father's chain of department stores single handed. Voluntary work, to a prospective employer, means that nobody was prepared to pay you for what you did. That's OK if you were a student gaining experience at the time, but, if not, you'd better have a good reason. Or leave it out.

◆ If your work is technical, IT related, for example, then use a **one-page summary CV** and attach back-up sheets with additional detail such as software and applications.

◆ **Summarise ambitions** and **key achievements** at the top and keep personal detail to a minimum. Write employment details in **date order**, with the most recent at the top.

◆ Prepare the other paperwork carefully and always **take copies** of your cover letters, references, application and interview forms to interviews with you. They can be a lifebelt in a tricky interview situation, saving you from contradicting yourself or from forgetting to raise key points.

◆ Give good reasons for leaving previous employment.

◆ Finally, before you finish with your CV, take a moment to **list** your own **personal selling points**. The positive ones are easy, but what about the negative ones? By this I mean the things that you take for granted about yourself but which stand out as defects in people who don't have them. Examples might be: **punctuality**, ability to **communicate** sympathetically, **honesty**, **efficiency-consciousness**,

profit-mindedness, loyalty. If you can't immediately think of examples, look at people who have been dismissed from your present or previous job. Why were they fired? Was it for a specific misdemeanour, or, more likely, because of poor timekeeping, frequent sick leave, low energy or a prickly disposition? Some personality traits go unnoticed in people who have them but can be impossible to work without in people who lack them. Nobody notices the person who regularly comes to work on time, but everybody notices when someone is late. Don't take anything about yourself for granted.

◆ Don't refer to anything that isn't on your CV. It's likely to make your interviewer query what else is missing.

Setting up a practice group

The best way to make sure you **excel** at interview is to **practise**. And you don't have to go to an expensive recruitment consultant to do that. Your local **Job Centre** may provide this service, or, if you currently work for a large organisation where redundancy is commonplace, there may be a **Career Action Centre** offering all kinds of job hunting help. And, if you are registered with recruitment agencies, look out for ones that provide interview skills training. Some do and some don't.

Your other alternative is to organise your own interview practice for free with the help of this book. You can do quite a bit yourself by **rehearsing questions** and **answers** in your mind and on paper. But it's much easier if you set up a **Practice Group** with some other job-seekers and work together on fine tuning your interview skills.

If you don't know anyone in the same boat (unlikely in today's economic climate!), and your family aren't prepared to take the exercise seriously enough to help you out, make a start anyway. Take the time to do this every day until you get the job you want. **Once is not enough.** For a start, you are unlikely to take it seriously yourself the first couple of times. No wonder you feel you don't do yourself justice in job interviews if you can't even impress yourself with your own performance.

What you need to be able to do is to put yourself into a **calm** and **confident** state at will. Think how great it would be if you could do that whenever you found yourself sitting in a reception area, waiting to be called in to interview. Think how great it would be if, instead of walking in with trembling hands and a blank mind, you could be **composed** and **resourceful**.

> 'It is extraordinary how extraordinary the ordinary person is.' George F. Will.

Sports psychologists use some simple but powerful techniques to put athletes into a **positive, winning**

frame of mind. These exercises can be useful in all stressful, competitive situations.

Step One Sit down and think back to an interview when you performed really well. It doesn't have to be a job interview. It could be a successful sale you made, a difficult situation you defused – even the romantic dinner when you proposed to your partner. This first step in your preparation is nothing to do with techniques, **it's about getting yourself into the right state**. Because, as you know, more interview opportunities are lost through nervousness than through lack of knowledge or expertise.

Step Two When you have a successful situation in mind, **run through it again**, picturing how you looked, what you wore, what you said and did. When you have that information, take it one step further and recall some of the feelings from that situation. What **emotions** were associated with that positive experience in your life? What **physical sensations** were there?

Step Three Check now whether you are an **observer**, watching your confident, successful, self giving a great performance, or whether you're actually right back there playing the role all over again.

Step Four If you're looking at yourself from the outside, try bringing the picture **closer**. If it's like looking at an old photograph, **put some life** into it. Put some colour into it and turn it into a movie.

Step Five When you're close enough, just step into it. Get right there into that experience again and **re-live it**.

Step Six Do this a few times. Go in and come out again. Train yourself to do it at will and, gradually, you will find you are able to **access** the **feelings** of **control** and **confidence** without having to go through the whole visualisation process first.

Rehearsing

Having taken some hints from sports psychology, we can also learn a lot about interviewing skills from the acting profession. Am I suggesting you shouldn't go into an interview and be yourself? Certainly not. Competent, qualified, people usually fail in interview simply because they are too nervous to be themselves and come across as too anxious to be employable. Most interviewers believe that a person who can't cope with an interview would be similarly incompetent in a stressful work situation.

Let's assume that you've managed to set up your Practice Group and you're ready to rehearse some interviews. The following techniques are useful ones in that sort of situation – and if you can use a video camera, it doubles the usefulness in terms of **feedback** to the interviewee.

> 'Make your mistakes in the company of friends,
> the audience won't give you a second chance.'
> Damien Harracks, The Performing Heart.

Most actors work with a script. But the script only works if it's so well rehearsed that it doesn't sound like one. The first thing to do is to write it, memorise it and practise it.

Prepare a *tell me about yourself* statement with six positive points:

1. I'm well qualified.
2. I've got lots of experience.
3. I'm well organised.
4. I have a good track record in this area.
5. I'm a good team leader.
6. I would fit into your organisation perfectly.

The next task is to make this catalogue of virtues sound totally convincing. Practise these statements over and over until they become **second nature** to you. Now try them out in front of your audience and ask for **feedback**. The fact that you will be doing the same for them usually makes this exercise a little less embarrassing. These are the answers you need to have:

- Do you believe me?

- What is it that gives me away? Is it my body language, my tone of voice, my eye contact (or lack of it)? Get some real detail here.

Of course a real interview isn't going to be like this. There aren't many situations when you get an uninterrupted opportunity to tell a prospective employer how wonderful you are (except in your CV). So invite your audience to **heckle**, or at least **interrupt** your flow and ask you **difficult** questions. There are some classic questions in Chapter 6.

Finally, ask for more detailed feedback.

- What are my strengths?

- What are my weaknesses?

- How is my image?

- What changes could I make?

Summary points

- **Check the job out carefully: have you really found out as much as you can? Do you know enough to be sure that you want it, that you have a chance of getting it, that you can ask well informed questions and can tailor your CV?**

◆ Tailor your CV: have you refined your CV so that you have a basic model with different trimmings? Or, if your career path is so tightly defined that the same CV will do for all applications, have you had someone else check it over for glitches and inconsistencies that might let you down in interview?

◆ Practice: put together a practice group. It's a useful way of working through many of the exercises in this book.

◆ Rehearse. Be disciplined about this – if you are currently unemployed, then job hunting should be your nine-to-five job, just to keep yourself in the working habit. Allocate an hour or so, either daily or weekly, to work with your practice group – or alone -- on your interview techniques. Lining up the prospects is great, but it's the interview that will get you the job.

Chapter 2

Psychometric Testing and Criteria-based Interviewing

'We all have ability. The difference is how we use it.'
Stevie Wonder

In this Chapter:

◆ **psychometric testing**

◆ **understanding psychometric tests**

◆ **making criteria-based interviewing work in your favour**

◆ **working on the criteria that count**

◆ **doing aptitude tests and job simulation exercises.**

The results of psychometric tests, handwriting tests and intelligence tests vary according to mood and test conditions. Practice won't raise your intelligence or stabilise your personality, but familiarity helps you stay calm enough to do yourself justice.

Ask what format the interview will take – this buys time to tune into the interviewer and unfamiliar surroundings. The interviewer may be nervous too, especially if there's a lot a stake. Fear of hiring the wrong person doesn't make for a relaxed, open-minded attitude. Inexperienced interviewers often try to cope by reverting to a social chat.

If you meet a skilled interviewer who is working to a set of criteria, you are lucky. They will give you the best chance to show what you can do and will be as keen to discover real talent as you are to display it. What's more, they will happily share their criteria with you and admire your pro-active attitude in asking.

Is this you?

- Do you regard an interview as a battle of wits?

- Are you always interviewed, but never selected?

- Do you freeze in interview?

- Or do you talk too much?

- Have you ever thought you'd do better if you knew what was going on in the interviewer's mind?

- Do you think you don't do yourself justice in interview and that's why you never get the chance to prove yourself in the job?

Psychometric testing

If you are serious about your job search, take yourself along to a Career Agency, get them to run you through all the most common and popular tests and give you

detailed feedback. Then, when you are presented with one of these tests in interview, you can tell the interviewer where you normally come on the scale. Most tests look for middle of the road, stable personalities and you are more likely to appear sane if you keep calm and *don't* try to analyse what the test is looking for. Just do it.

Some of the common ones are Myers Briggs (MBTI), Saville & Holdsworth, Occupational Personality Quotient (S.H.L.O.P.Q), the Sixteen Personality Factors (16PF) and Thomas International – but if you're comfortable with the general idea, you needn't be fazed by one of the many others you might come across.

> 'Self Trust is the first secret of success.' Ralph Waldo Emerson.

If you are given a handwriting test, an intelligence test – or even asked for your time of birth – there is nothing you can do to change the basic data. But you can make sure that you're clear and relaxed so you give your best possible result. There are a number of exercises that will help you to put yourself in the right state every time (see Chapter 5).

Understanding psychometric tests

Psychometric testing is simply a standardised, and

hopefully objective, way of measuring various aspects of mental performance. They should be administered by appropriately trained staff under carefully controlled conditions, and the results assessed against previously calculated average scores.

There are two main types of psychometric testing.

1. Ability and aptitude testing

Ability (or IQ) tests measure your ability to learn and retain skills and information. Attainment tests are a subdivision of ability tests which measure what you have already learned and what you can do.

Sometimes the difference between ability testing and aptitude testing can seem a bit blurred, but in fact ability is a more general measurement than aptitude, which is more closely job related. Aptitude tests measure suitability for particular tasks and ways of thinking, and they are often designed for very specific jobs like the Programmers Aptitude Series for IT personnel.

Apparently up to 50 human abilities can be measured by psychometric tests, but in practice the focus is on about eight:

◆ **Abstract**
   This is about general reasoning and problem-solving abilities. Abstract reasoning tests usually involve sequences of symbols arranged in rows of squares. To

solve them you need to identify the different symbols
and what they have in common, identify the pattern
and finally predict the next part of the sequence.
These are IQ or ability tests and are used in most
tests.

◆ **Verbal**
These range from grammar and spelling to testing
your ability to understand verbal or written
information. These tests are very widely used in all
office-based occupations and employers like them
because they give a good indication of the employee's
ability to cope with the basics of communication.

◆ **Numerical**
These tests usually cover addition, subtraction,
multiplication and division and they involve number
sequences and the use of numerical data to solve
problems. They are most likely to be a part of
aptitude testing in the case of clerical jobs which are
likely to involve the use of numbers.

◆ **Perceptual**
These, again, are largely used as aptitude tests to select
people who would be best in scientific, engineering,
design and technical positions. It's unlikely that you'd
be applying for this kind of job unless you already
know you have some aptitude for it, but there's no
harm in practising. You can buy books of these tests
from Morrisby and Saville & Holdsworth, and you can
set yourself tasks of producing diagrams which explain
how your household systems such as your video

recorder works or drawing up strategic diagrams for winning board games.

◆ **Spatial**

Apparently 5% of the population are unable to manipulate 3-dimensional objects in their mind and these tests are less often used. However, they do give a good indication of whether people would be good at computer aided design and good spatial awareness is important for engineers, designers, architects and surveyors. The tests usually consist of pictures of shapes which may or may not be manipulated into 3D designs.

◆ **Mechanical**

These are very specifically used to assess people for more practical jobs and they are designed to test working knowledge of mechanical and physical principles. If you think this kind of knowledge is relevant and may be tested in the kind of job you're going for it would be a good idea to check that you understand the principles involved. GCSE level physics and technology textbooks are good sources of this kind of information.

2. Personality testing

There's no right and wrong answers with personality testing – it's about how you do things rather than what you can do. Very often they are used at the beginning of the selection procedure as part of the screening progress with ability and aptitude tests being used later.

Personality testing can be as useful for you as for your prospective employers. If you could do with some help in deciding exactly what kind of career is right for you it would probably be helpful for you to take some personality tests on your own account and see what sort of work would be most satisfying and fulfilling for you.

The two basic types of personality test are:

1. Personality types
These questionnaires are designed to pick out the predictable differences in the ways people will behave in different circumstances. People are generally grouped into the following categories:

♦ **extroversion-introversion**

♦ **judging-perceiving**

♦ **sensing-intuition**

♦ **thinking-feeling.**

The questionnaires themselves are usually presented as **forced choice** or **ranking** questions.

A forced choice question might be:

Do you prefer to:
♦ Plan what you do in advance?

♦ React to things as they happen?

A ranking question might be:

Rank in order of interest (a to b) the following pastimes:
- ◆ Going to the cinema.

- ◆ Reading.

- ◆ Going to a restaurant with friends.

Personality type questionnaires are useful for showing the kind of environments in which people prefer to work, the way they approach their work and the kind of personalities they work with best.

2. Personality traits
These questionnaires are designed to measure up to 30 or more personality traits but most of them concentrate on five core traits.

- ◆ action
- ◆ thinking
- ◆ relating
- ◆ feeling
- ◆ conformity.

Personality trait questionnaires come in two basic formats: rating lists of statements or choosing between statements.

A rating question might be:

Circle (1) if you strongly agree with the following statement, (2) if you agree (3) if you don't know, (4) if you disagree and (5) if you strongly disagree.

◆ I like parties (1) (2) (3) (4) (5).

◆ I always keep appointments on time (1) (2) (3) (4) (5).

◆ I enjoy taking risks (1) (2) (3) (4) (5).

◆ I avoid competitive activities (1) (2) (3) (4) (5).

A choice question might be:

Indicate which statement is most like you (M) and which is least like you, (L). Leave the rest blank.

◆ I am very conscientious about my work (M) (L).

◆ I am very sociable (M) (L).

◆ I never let people down (M) (L).

◆ I like to get things done (M) (L).

Another choice format is:

Indicate whether the following statements are true (T) or false (F).

◆ I like organising meetings (T) (F).

◆ I always attend to the details (T) (F).

◆ I can usually see the big picture (T) (F).

◆ I'm not afraid to speak my mind (T) (F).

A third popular choice format is:

> Indicate whether the following statements are true (T), false (F), or if you're not sure (?).

- ◆ I don't like having to address large groups (T) (?) (F).

- ◆ I am more productive when I work in a team (T) (?) (F).

- ◆ I do best in leadership roles (T) (?) (F).

- ◆ I can control my feelings in difficult situations (T) (?) (F).

Remember that you can't cheat on personality tests and if you try to second-guess the answers you'll probably trip yourself up. However, these tests do reflect mood as well as personality so if you want to do well, practise getting yourself into a calm and logical frame of mind. Stress, anger or anxiety may show up and they are not qualities that most employers would want in an employee.

Test format

- ◆ A question and answer book in which you write down the answers alongside the questions.

- ◆ A palm top computer or a PC with a question book so that you read the questions from the book and enter the answers on the keyboard.

◆ A PC which gives you the questions and also the space to type in the answers.

In future there are likely to be multimedia tests with text, sound, video clips and movement, but these are still at the testing stage.

Tips for tests

◆ Practise as many types of test as you can in advance of the interview and train yourself to enjoy them – like doing a crossword puzzle or some other game you would normally have fun with.

◆ Practise some breathing exercises (see Chapter 5) so that you can use them to stay calm when you're actually presented with the tests in an interview.

◆ During the test, ask questions *before* the test starts if you don't know what's going on.

◆ Read the instructions carefully and think before you start filling anything in.

◆ Don't waste time on questions you can't answer or don't understand. Fill in all the obvious answers and then go back to the others at the end if you have time.

Common tests

There are thousands of tests on the market, most of them designed for English-speaking countries. In practice, there are a few you are more likely to come across than others.

♦ McQuaig.

♦ The Morrisby Profile (12 different tests measuring a range of different aptitudes and work-based personality).

♦ Raven's Progressive Matrices – abstract reasoning tests.

♦ Watson Glaser Critical Thinking Appraisal (verbal reasoning).

♦ ASE Graduate and Managerial Assessment (have a good verbal reasoning component).

♦ The Keirsey temperament sorter.

♦ Myers-Briggs personality test.

♦ Psytech International Ltd – Jung Type Indicator.

♦ Selby Millsmith Ltd – Occupational Type Profile.

♦ Enneagram personality test.

♦ Modern Occupational Skills Tests: Numerical Awareness, Numerical Estimation.

♦ The Test Agency Shapes Analysis Test.

You may be able to get more information about some of these tests on the Internet but the ones listed below are definitely available for sampling.

Tests available for sampling on the Internet

♦ Saville and Holdsworth is one of the main UK producers of recruitment tests and they can give you some sample questions and advice on preparing for tests online. In addition to sample questions, there are practice tests, but there is an online charge for these.

◆ Civil Service tests – you can download these. (You must be familiar with downloading information to a file, then opening that file.) Similar tests are available as a reference booklet in CDU.

◆ Mensa tests – check out the Mensa website.

◆ Criterion Partnership.

◆ SHL Direct – includes some useful advice on preparing for these tests. The tests used in the CDU workshops are produced by SHL.

◆ Nfer-Nelson.

◆ Ratol.

◆ Kaplan.

◆ Tests, Tests, Tests.

◆ Traditional IQ Tests.

◆ Brain Tainment centre.

◆ Assessment Systems Ltd.

Further information

The British Psychological Society, St Andrews House, 48 Princess Road East, Leicester LE1 7DR. Tel: (0116) 254 9568. Fax: (0116) 247 0787. email: enquiry~bps.org.uk

Making criteria-based interviewing work in your favour

Ask, when you make the appointment, if it will be a criteria-based interview. If the answer is yes, find out what the criteria are. Even if it's not as formal as this, always ask exactly what **personal qualities**, **skills** and **experience** the employer is looking for. Then you can **update** your CV so that it shows you have the right stuff and you can run a mind search for instances of past behaviour to fit each criterion.

A good interviewer knows that the best predictor of future behaviour is past behaviour. They will be asking you questions aimed at finding out what you have done in past jobs (and other) situations. A poor interviewer will ask leading questions like *I suppose you're a people person?* Questions like this seem like a gift because they give you the answer, but in fact they lower the standard of the interview so that poorer candidates are harder to weed out.

> 'The secret of all victory lies in the organisation of the non-obvious.' Oswald Spengler.

Good criteria-based interviewing **focuses** on the **job**, not the **person**. This sounds harsh, but there wouldn't be an interview if there wasn't a job. In times of high unemployment job interviews are not ego pampering experiences. Talking about your own needs and interests is counter productive, you need to be **thinking** of yourself – and **reinventing** yourself if necessary – in terms of the organisation you're applying to join.

You can define the criteria this way. **Job Description/ Task Analysis + Person Specification = Criteria.** Remember the Zoo Keeper?

Job Description	**Person Specification**
Cleaning out cages of large cats.	Hard worker, able to cope with messy, possibly dangerous job.
Feeding large cats.	Knowledge of very specific dietary requirements and ability to handle raw meat.
Ensuring that large cats are healthy (they are harder and more expensive to replace than their keepers).	Some expert knowledge and keen powers of observation.
Ensuring that cages are secure and the public is safe.	Attention to detail and powers of observation.
Ensuring that the public is well informed. Without the paying public there is no zoo and no job.	Likes people, and animals, ability to communicate.
Ensuring that zoo management and fellow keepers are well informed.	Knowledge of hierarchy and ability to communicate. Needs to be a team player.

Criteria

1. Experience of working with animals
2. Good communicator
3. Attention to detail
4. Physically fit

When you have all the information you can **gather** about the job and you've either been given the criteria or worked them out for yourself, **organise** your **skills** and **experience** to fit. You can supplement direct work experience with examples from other areas of your life.

You may never have had anything to do with tigers before, but a background in **security**, together with some **fitness training** in your spare time and **volunteer work** at an **animal rescue** charity would all be relevant and would demonstrate most of the criteria. Many other life experience combinations would do the same.

Working on the criteria that count

Start work on the interview before you apply for the job. Get your **strengths** and **weaknesses** down on paper – then you can tailor yourself to the requirements of a particular job. If you concentrate on the three main areas which concern most interviewers, you can easily pre-prepare some strong, positive, behavioural examples for each area of your life.

◆ **Biographical:** evidence of your ability to do a particular job might include experience of living abroad, familiarity with a particular environment or lifestyle, or proven flexibility in living patterns.

◆ **Technical:** measurable expertise, including specific qualifications, degrees, certificates, training programmes or experience in a particular area.

◆ **Behavioural:** gathering evidence from friends, family and self analysis will help you take yourself apart ready for re-assembly according to a particular job specification. This exercise works both ways. It can help you persuade an interviewer that you are suitable for a particular job, but may also help you check in advance whether that job is suitable for you.

When you have reviewed these areas of your life, you can run a **practice interview** by going through the following questions and substituting answers of your own. These are some of the most common criteria that employers use but you may be aware of others that would apply to your particular industry – flexibility perhaps, decision making, planning or reliability. List them and think of some questions – get your Practice Group to help – then work on some good answers you can use in interview.

The following are examples of the most **frequently used criteria** and some **typical questions**:

Drive and Motivation
Q Tell me about a time when you worked hard but felt a great sense of achievement.

A When planning permission for the new office development was turned down, I carried out another round of consultation and I drew up new plans. At the third attempt, amended plans were accepted and the offices were built.

Communication and Negotiating Skills

Q Do you think problems are solved by better communication?

A During the strike I talked to the staff about what they really wanted. It turned out they were more worried about redundancy than pay. I got management to give them the facts on the threat from our nearest rival and they agreed to a productivity deal.

Interpersonal Skills

Q What unpopular decisions have you made?

A I believe that the benefits of unpopular decisions have to be sold to the people they affect, otherwise they won't work. Recently the tea lady retired and we were going to install a machine on every floor. I called a staff meeting first and discovered people were already grumbling about the system being too impersonal. So we asked them what would work and they voted for a small coffee bar.

Energy

Q Give an example of when you did more than was required.

A When we set up the first self learning groups for employees to develop their business skills, I joined the first three groups myself and went to every meeting to show my commitment.

Honesty/Integrity
Q Are you trustworthy?

A My current line manager now leaves me to oversee both payroll and purchasing, at the recent audit our department had the lowest number of discrepancies.

Coping with Stress
Q How do you handle stress?

A I work well under stress and I'm good at switching off completely when I need to. In my last job I ran stress management classes for some of the junior executives.

Effort/Initiative
Q Tell me about a project you started.

A Our turnover was falling so I organised a monthly training update programme for the sales staff.

Problem Solving
Q Can you think of a time when you solved a problem where others had failed?

A I was moved to the overseas office to manage a difficult but creative team who didn't want management imposed on them. I solved the problem by making it a two way process, they were to train me in their system at the same time that I was teaching them the new procedures.

Efficiency

Q What's your attitude to efficiency versus staff satisfaction?

A I don't believe there's a conflict. If the system works smoothly it's better for everyone. But if the system isn't user friendly, that in itself leads to resentment and more inefficiency.

Leadership

Q Do you see yourself as a leader or a follower?

A There are always people I can learn from. But when I am in a position of responsibility I enjoy taking the lead. Although this will be my first big promotion, I was elected chairman of the PTA at my children's school three years ago and built up the fund raising committee to raise money for a new swimming pool.

This perfect employee could probably take over from Richard Branson, but you don't have to come up with a real example for every heading yourself. See which ones you find examples for most **easily**. That in itself will tell you quite a lot – about yourself and your ideal job.

It's hard work but if you don't do it in advance, you'll be

hard put to come up with anything convincing in the five to ten seconds you get in interview to describe how you dealt with a difficult employee or improved sales figures.

> 'Learn to be flexible, it makes the curves in your life path much easier to manoeuvre.' Cherie Carter-Scott.

Sometimes, when you have the skills and experience, it's frustrating when the right questions don't crop up. Help the interviewer by volunteering the information anyway: 'I see that this job requires someone who's very flexible and that's something I'm good at. For example...'

Here are some do's and don'ts.

◆ **Pick out** what you've been told (or what you think) are the **key criteria** for the job you're considering. Then see how many relevant illustrations of those criteria you can come up with from your list. If you can't find any at all, maybe it's not the job for you.

◆ Even if interviewers aren't using a formal criteria-based interview system, they love being given this kind of **behavioural evidence**. It can also be useful if you are asked to make an impromptu presentation on a work related topic.

◆ Criteria-based interview questions require more than one-word answers. If somebody asks what exactly you do in your current job, don't just say you work for the accounts department. They don't want irrelevant details about where you eat lunch, but they do want an **overview** of your **responsibilities** and **challenges**.

◆ **Don't generalise** – this frustrates the skilful interviewer. Keep generalisations for times when you have to fudge and you really need them. Don't waste them when you have real answers.

◆ Don't be nervous if an interviewer is taking notes. Make it easy for them – give them **succinct soundbites** that they can't resist writing down. Then it's your version that gets recorded.

Doing aptitude tests and job simulation exercises

Many jobs now give on-the-spot tests, such as **in-tray exercises** for administrative posts, or a **walk-about** for a security position. At senior levels, candidates are often given problems to solve. Don't be caught out – you may not be warned in advance, but, given an interview time exceeding one hour, you can safely assume there will be a **hands on** situation.

> 'Focused action beats brilliance any day.' Art Turock.

If you think this is likely, **prepare in advance**. If there is some element of the work which is less familiar to you, or which you haven't done for some time, go through it in your mind. The brain processes this kind of activity in just the same way as the real thing. **Mental practice** is often as useful as hands on experience.

Here's some useful tips for in-tray tests:

◆ **Sort** first, then **prioritise** with sticky notes (take some with you).

◆ **Resignations** and **people issues** are always top priority.

◆ Expect **important** details to be near the **bottom**.

◆ Work through in the **order** you decided.

◆ Make an **action list**, including telephone calls or emails. Minimise memos.

Summary points

◆ Psychometric testing is impersonal, so there's nothing you can do about the results – except make sure you are in the calmest, clearest state to do yourself justice.

◆ Make criteria-based interviewing work in your favour by checking out or working out the criteria in advance.

◆ Prepare the evidence to show that you can match up to the criteria.

◆ **Aptitude tests and job simulation exercises favour experienced candidates. Putting yourself in a steady, focused frame of mind is the key to success.**

Chapter 3

Establishing Rapport with the Interviewer

'Who do they choose? At the end of the day, they choose the guy they like the best'. Jay Abrahams

In this Chapter:

◆ **opening moves**
◆ **using representational systems to communicate fast**
◆ **pacing and leading**
◆ **observing the basic body language rule.**

In spite of using every kind of test, from IQ to EQ (and even astrological analysis in one US company) **rapport** still counts for a lot. In the current job market, with many well qualified applicants chasing the same vacancy, the interviewer is likely to pick the candidate he feels most **comfortable** with.

Unfortunately, a lot of good applicants are screened out this way. They communicate well in their familiar work and social groups, but in interview they're nervous. They try to be efficient rather than warm and they don't put themselves across as well as they could. Communicating upwards without grovelling or being pushy is a skill that can be learned. There are plenty of useful techniques used in sales training and many other business applications.

Is this you?

◆ Are you uncomfortable with people who are senior to you in status?

◆ Do you find it difficult to relax and be open with authority figures?

◆ Are you stiff and even sometimes a little aggressive?

◆ Or excessively quiet and unassertive?

◆ Do you wish you could form quick and easy working relationships so that you could be at your most quick-witted and likeable when the job you really want is at stake?

Opening moves

As you walk into the interview room, be **aware** of your surroundings and the person (or people) waiting for you. This takes you out of yourself, makes you **less self-conscious** and gives you **advance information** about the **tone**, **mood** and **style** of the interview.

Photograph the whole room, the chairs, the light and the people, in your mind. This prevents the details of the surroundings from distracting you, and you will automatically know where to place yourself.

Adopt a five point protocol. Don't waste time dithering over basics. In an hour or less, you don't have time to waste. **Learn the rules**, stick with them and save your on-the-spot decision making for important issues, like asking the right questions and answering the questions right.

> 'If you want to pull a rabbit out of a hat, make sure you put one in there first.'

Hardwire the following points into your brain and you'll gain five minutes of useful time at the beginning of any interview or formal meeting.

◆ **Smile**, make **eye contact** and **shake hands**.

◆ Wait to be **invited** to sit. Take the seat indicated or ask where to sit. If given a choice, get your back to the light, but **don't flap about it**.

◆ Even if you are invited to smoke, **don't** do it.

◆ Address your interviewer **formally** unless invited to use first names.

◆ Always accept a **glass of water** or a **cup of coffee**. It's useful if your throat gets dry and it gives you something to fiddle with. You don't have to drink it.

Using representational systems to communicate fast

We experience the world and other people through our senses or representational systems. For practical purposes this means **sight** and **sound**. Touch and smell are less important – if you become aware of either touch or smell in a business situation, it's probably a bad sign. We take our representational systems for granted, but we can improve their efficiency at least 70% by becoming more consciously aware of what our senses are telling us.

Although we all use all our senses (unless we are deaf or visually impaired), everybody has favourites. The human being who gets information equally from all the senses is rare. And the human being who communicates equally in all the sensory languages is even rarer – people who do that naturally are great communicators (and terrific salespersons).

> 'Whenever I go into a difficult situation I imagine I'm an alien getting out of the spaceship and into a new environment – I have imaginary antenna processing every little bit of information to help me survive.' Bilal Hadari.

Awareness of our sensory systems is important in two ways:

◆ **Information In:** practise using all your senses more fully, particularly your **sight** and **hearing** and you will pick up a lot more useful information. Most importantly, the interviewer will be showing you how they want you to communicate with them and what style of organisation you are dealing with. There's a lot you won't be told in so many words – but you can pick it up anyway.

◆ **Information Out:** the more information you have about how another person communicates, the more easily you will be able to tune in to them and speak their language. This means you can put across more **information** about yourself much more **quickly**. A lot of what we say to strangers is wasted because we haven't bothered to translate it into their language. There's no time in an interview for communications that don't hit the target.

Verbal rapport is the most effective and direct way of tuning in to someone else. We'll discuss the visual messages, or body language, at the end of the chapter. The **words** people **use** are the most important clue to their preferred sensory style of communication. But the interviewer will only be speaking for 15% of the time or less, which doesn't give you much time to pick up both the meaning and the style of what they're saying to you.

Everyone uses **auditory**, **visual** and **kinaesthetic** language but most people communicate in one system more than the others. You can assume that the way people express themselves is the way they most easily understand. The style of language interviewers use indicates the way they want you to **feed** information back. They will give you clues about their preferred choice of language as soon as they open their mouth.

Visual people use a whole spectrum of **highly visual** expressions. They'll want to look at this, show you that, **focus** on their perspective and envisage a bright future. They remember things **visually**. If they talk about putting you in the picture and giving you a clearer idea of what the job is about, you will break rapport if you tell them it **sounds** interesting. **I see what you mean** is a more appropriate response.

Most people are primarily visual – but don't assume that everybody is that way. Auditory people put the accent on **harmony**, turn a **deaf ear** to **dumb ideas** and tell you they want someone who is on their **wavelength**. If that rings a bell with you, and you strike the right note with them, you may get a job offer.

Feelings people or **kinaesthetics** will warm to you if you can give them a feel for what you might be like as a colleague and if you are a comfortable person to be with. Kinaesthetic people are rarer, but if you come across one, you have to make them think you'll fit in well and that you are a strong candidate.

A lot of people are uncomfortable with these ideas, because they don't seem like hard facts. But you won't last in a job where you can't **communicate comfortably** with your boss – however well qualified you are.

Don't expect to become aware of other people's communication styles (or even your own) overnight. But **perseverance** does make for **progress**. Here are a few simple exercises you can run through with your Interview Practice Group.

Check out your own bias by getting someone to give you a topic to talk about for one minute using a particular representational system. You could talk about the weather, but it's more useful to pick a subject that might actually arise in interview. Something like 'the task I dislike', 'my greatest achievement', 'time management', 'goal setting'.

Ask your practice partner to give you a subject **relevant** to your own job search and tell you what language to use. Imagine you are asked to talk for a couple of minutes about filing, using auditory language. You might start like this:

'Filing sounds like a boring job, but I always hear warning bells when my desk starts to get chaotic, so I just tell myself to get on with it. That works for me and it stops my secretary shouting at me. Once my desk is clear, I can hear myself think again.'

While you talk, your partner notes every word you use that fits the criteria. You won't need much **feedback** because you will soon know if a particular system is **easy** or **difficult** for you. You will very likely find that one representational system comes much more naturally to you than another.

For example, you might be totally at home with visual language:

'When I see my desk covered in paper and I'm spending ages looking for the things I need, I know it's time to do the filing. If there's clutter everywhere I look, I can't even get my priorities for the day clear in my mind.'

Or you might be more at home with kinaesthetic, or feeling, terminology:

'When my desk is in a muddle it makes me feel edgy and inefficient. I'm sharper and I feel more on top of things if it's all in the right place and I know just where to put my hand on what I need.'

Listen to how other people communicate by trying the same exercise out on the friend who's been helping you. Get more people involved so that you get to know a greater range of styles.

When you experience these systems in action, you will realise how powerful this is. That's when the value of learning to be observant and flexible will become more apparent to you.

See how easy it is to alter your own preferred system.
How much more flexible can you become? Whenever
you speak to anyone for the next week or so, make a
conscious effort to notice how they say what they say
and experiment with speaking their language.

**Feel what it's like to tune into the speech patterns of
others.** Watch more TV, particularly the **news** and **chat**
shows. When someone asks a question, think about the
language they are using as well as the content of the
message, and think how you might answer those
questions yourself. Listen carefully to the interviewee's
responses and give them marks out of ten. This is fun to
do and you will soon feel like an expert. Then it's time to
start practising on your family and friends. Reading about
interview skills is only the first step to practising them
before actually putting them into practice.

As you become more skilful at speaking other people's
language, notice what a difference it makes to your daily
transactions. One of the most important findings of
Neuro Linguistic Programming is that tuning into
another person's speech patterns is the key to successful
communication. And it seems to be equally effective in
business, social and therapeutic settings.

If you are trying to sell someone your skills and they tell
you that they're looking for a person to share their
vision for the company, someone who sees the broader
picture and keeps a balanced perspective on market
trends, you don't reply

'I hear what you're saying, let me tell you about my background – it's pretty much in tune with what you're looking for.'

That's a mismatch in language terms and it will break rapport.

Don't underestimate this **conscious** use of **language patterns**. It's powerful enough to be considered unethical by organisations who don't want to invest their money in training their sales staff to use it. In interview, you are making the most important sale of your life – your own skills in return for a salary.

These aren't skills you can switch on and off. With practice they will become part of your daily transactional repertoire. Think how useful they could be in all the areas of your life – we are always being interviewed for something, whether it's money or love. We are always trying to sell somebody something.

Pacing and leading

Imagine yourself in the interview room. You've practised your **language skills**, you're **perceptive** and **flexible**, but, despite all your preparation, everything seems to be happening just a bit too fast. You're anxious about not getting your points across, so your breathing rate increases as your brain seems to slow down and you feel yourself blushing as your hand rattles the coffee cup.

What can you do? You can **slow it down**. Don't assume that the interviewer controls the pace. It's usually up for grabs. Take it to the **level** which enables you to make your **best impression** – unless of course your natural pace is irritatingly slow or fast (something you need to know in advance – ask your Practice Group).

Slow things down by using your voice, but always start at the interviewer's pace. If you want to take somebody somewhere, you have to start from where they are. Don't speak **slowly** for no apparent reason because that is nothing but **annoying**. **Match the speed** of your **gestures** and **voice** to the interviewer and gradually ease down to a manageable speed. This could be a great relief to the interviewer if you are the third or fourth interviewee of the day. He is probably in overdrive – so bored with his set-piece speech that he's saying it too fast and pushing up his own stress levels.

'The most important trip you may take in life is meeting people halfway.' Earl J Montrose.

If you can **moderate** the **pace** a little so that you can make appropriate, relevant responses, the interviewer will also be aware of a certain **relief** and feeling of **comfort** in your presence. This will reflect positively in the write-up you get at the end of the session.

On the other hand, you may get a semi-comatose interviewer who is demotivating you and sending you to sleep. If that happens, **reverse** the **procedure**. Don't pitch straight in at a fast pace, you'll look pushy and make the interviewer tense and edgy. Start **slowly**, match the low energy to begin with and speed up **gradually** – you will notice the interviewer's level of interest rise with your own.

Observing the basic body language rule

There is one basic rule about body language in an interview situation:

Always be guided by the cues the interviewer gives you.

This is one area where you let the interviewer set the pace. You want them to stay within their natural comfort zone. This rule applies to **personal space, eye contact**, **touching** and **posture** and will save you from agonising about the correct footage of personal space and the number of seconds of eye contact.

But, before you attempt to mirror someone else, make sure you are **aware** of your own **natural pace** and **patterns**. The practice sessions we mentioned in Chapter 1 are useful. Watch TV interviews, take special notice of appearance, body language and the believability of gestures. When you think you are ready, you can start practising body language on other people.

'Learn to be intense without being tense.' Joe
Torre, Baseball Manager.

A warm smile and a cool demeanour always helps. If
you know you are a naturally touchy, feely person who
likes to get close to others, **make sure you don't do it
in an interview**. However, if the interviewer gets closer
to you than the standard 4 to 6 feet, hold your ground
(unless you are actually being harassed). Backing off will
be interpreted as a negative signal.

According to the famous Mehrabian pie chart, **body
language** is of **primary importance** in any encounter,
with **tone of voice** second and **content** coming a poor
third. This may be truer for social gatherings than
business situations.

Body language is certainly **important**, but probably not
as overwhelmingly important as the writers of
complicated books on the subject would have us believe.
Which is just as well. You have plenty to think about
without consciously analysing your interviewer's body
language. It was never meant to be interpreted by the
conscious mind because it is far too complex for the
conscious mind to cope with. Is he crossing his arms
because he's resistant to what you are saying? Or because
he's cold? Or because he finds you threatening? Or
because he finds you overwhelmingly attractive and is
trying to retain self control? Your conscious mind won't

be able to tell the difference, but your subconscious will. Which is why you should free your conscious mind to deal with what it does best – like answering complicated questions about your attitude to team management.

Summary points

◆ **Opening moves matter, but if you memorise the basics you will save precious time and energy for the real focus of the interview.**

◆ **Using representational systems to communicate fast is the best route to rapport and the most effective way of communicating your skills.**

◆ **Pacing and leading the interviewer will put you in control of the interview so that you can regulate the pace and put your points across comfortably.**

◆ **The basic body language rule is to take your cue from the interviewer – don't try to analyse it.**

Chapter 4

Thinking On Your Feet

'Test fast. Fail fast. Adjust fast.' Tom Peters

In this Chapter:
- **buying time/buying signals**
- **asking questions**
- **controlling the content**
- **taking notes**
- **listening skills.**

An interview is a sales pitch and you are the product. Unless your skills and experience are in short supply, in which case you will be interviewing your prospective employers, rather than vice versa. But, if you are just one of many well-qualified and experienced applicants for the same few jobs, you will have to do some competitive selling.

You may say *'I'm not a salesman, I'm a Project Designer, a Teacher, an Accounts Executive...'* but we are all in the business of sales. We are always selling something: an idea, a relationship, a product.

If you have the intention of actively selling your skills,

you will feel more in control. And most people feel better and perform better when they have some control. Of course there will be surprises and unexpected questions, but there are many ways of staying in command: by asking questions, by actively listening, and by taking notes so that you can refer back to difficult points.

Is this you?

♦ Does the knowledge that you are just one of many well-qualified candidates for every job make you feel powerless in interview?

♦ Do you feel uncomfortable and incompetent when you're under pressure in unfamiliar surroundings?

♦ Do you find it hard to ask questions when you are intimidated?

♦ When you walk out of an interview, do you sometimes have the feeling that you were caught wrong footed and you didn't do yourself justice – simply because it was all happening faster than you were able to think?

Buying time/buying signals

Awareness of some **basic sales techniques** can take you beyond feeling comfortable in interview and on into enjoyment of the adrenaline rush and challenge of the situation.

Selling the benefits is the most important sales technique of all. Every salesperson knows that they have to sell the **benefit** of the product rather than the product itself. The interviewer is not interested in you as a well-rounded person. The interviewer is trying to fit you into a slot in the organisation and if you can demonstrate that you are the **right size** and **shape** for that particular slot you have much more chance of getting the job. Trying to put across all your good points without regard for the employer's requirements may distract the interviewer from the direct benefits you have to offer.

'Know your price, get out there and sell!' Mae-Belle Monroe.

You must decide what to sell. Analysing the criteria for a job will have given you a pretty good idea of the benefits you need to sell. Nevertheless, it's important to listen carefully in interview for **live, on-the-spot clues**.

If the interviewer is the person you'll be working with, the first thing they'll tell you is what kind of **language** you need to use to get through to them (Chapter 3). And they will also tell you exactly what sort of person they are looking for – if you listen carefully.

You may think you will get a job by what you say in interview. But **listening** is actually more important than talking – if you don't listen carefully you may **answer** the **wrong questions** – or give the **wrong answers** to the right ones.

Leading the interviewer can bring positive results. There are two reasons for asking questions:

◆ to get more information about the job

◆ to get a 'yes' response. This puts the interviewer into a **positive thinking mode** which is much more likely to lead them into a buying (hiring) position. For example:

'Would it be true to say that you are you looking for somebody who will be a good team player?'

Once you are getting consistent yes responses, you can slip in some questions which start from the premise that you are already an employee:

'If I were to join you, what would my first assignment be?'

Without thinking about it, the interviewer will already be allocating your first task to you and picturing you doing it.

When you have got the interviewer to the point where they are seriously considering you as a potential employee, how do you recognise the buying signals and capitalise on it? There are two indications:

◆ When the interviewer starts to ask you leading questions based on the assumption that you are appointed, for example, 'Would you be happy with a corner office?' or 'When could you start?'

◆ When the interviewer's body language changes from negative to positive.

Negative	Positive
Leaning back or crossing arms	Suddenly rubbing the chin
Fiddling with a watch or fingernail	Index finger on cheek
Clenching hands	Leaning forward
Pulling an ear	Rubbing hands

Asking questions

It's as important to **ask** the **right questions** as to **answer** the **questions right**. An interview with questions and answers flying both ways is generally more comfortable for everybody than one which consists solely of the job applicant being grilled by the employer. And, if the interviewer is comfortable, that's good for the interviewee. When you feel **at ease** in an interview, your interviewer will usually be **relaxed** as well. A situation that feels awkward, even if you can't put your finger on exactly why, often means that rapport has not been established.

Asking questions gives you **control** and **breathing space**.

What do you want? is the most obvious question. If the active listening hasn't done the trick, ask the interviewer **directly** what they are looking for. Then you can pick the appropriate parts of your own experience (they don't have to be job related, but they must be **relevant**). There's no rule against asking direct questions and no prize for being unnecessarily devious.

Advanced information is obtained by asking factual questions. They buy time and make you look intelligent – much better than just wasting time with irrelevant queries. Interview time is short, so give specifics and get specifics.

'In time of drastic change, it is the learners who inherit the future. Those who have finished learning find themselves equipped to live in a world that no longer exists.' Eric Hoffer.

There's no substitute for doing your **homework** and being totally **up to date** with your potential employer and the company situation. If there has been something in the news that week, or, better still, that morning, mention it. If you don't want to risk a comment, keep it neutral. Don't commit yourself to an opinion. By doing so you still get the benefit of looking aware and well informed.

Remember there's a **difference** between asking **educated** and **interested** questions and telling someone how to **run** their business. The latter approach is never well received and you need to know the difference between being **pro-active** and **aggressive**.

Multi purpose questions are always welcome. Interviewers like to be asked questions because it shows that the candidate is interested in the job. Sometimes an interviewer will even close by saying 'Well, I expect there are some questions you want to ask?' And, when this happens, there's nothing worse than being caught out and saying 'Well, actually, I think you've covered everything.'

There are some great multi-purpose questions you can prepare in advance:

- ◆ Is there a written job description?
- ◆ What kind of performance appraisal systems do you have here?
- ◆ Would there be opportunities for growth in this organisation?
- ◆ Is there provision for training?

Save the worst 'til last. Ask about pay, conditions, equal rights, benefits etc. at the end. It gives a bad impression if you seem over-concerned about them at the beginning.

Controlling the content

Focus your mind on your strong points, not your weak ones. Don't try to distract the interviewer from your weak points by waffling – if you really haven't got enough benefits to sell, maybe this isn't the job for you.

Prepare your primary focus areas in advance, but be prepared not to use all of them. If parts of your experience are **irrelevant** to a potential employer, **let them go**. They are only benefits if the employer needs them and if they aren't benefits, don't try to sell them.

The **preparation** rule applies to anything you might refer to in the interview. If you are asked about current events, films or books, pick a few very recent ones and make sure you have some **informed opinions** about them. Believe it or not, people often mention books that they haven't read and films they haven't seen.

Use your **CV** in the interview. Refer to it whenever you feel you might be losing your way. You wrote it, so you can use it as a means of getting back on track and staying in **control**. Interviewers like talking through a CV – they can make notes on it and refer back to it afterwards. A **well-written** CV gives you lots of hooks for mini-presentations about your **good points** and **achievements**.

> 'Passion is everything.' David Copperfield.

Take into account the halo effect and use it to your advantage. It's not very British to boast, we tend to play down our achievements and play up our mistakes. Don't do this in an interview. One **solid achievement** will **overshadow** a lot of mediocrity and a mistake or two as well.

Taking notes

Whatever the interview style, take with you the paperwork, your CV and the mindset that gives you the best possible chance.

◆ **Pen and paper:** whether or not the interviewer is taking notes, there are good reasons why you should. When the interviewer is talking, you can note down your next question so that you don't have to hold it in your mind. This way your brain is clear to focus on the nuances of the conversation. In spite of the fact that you will be expected to talk for 85% of the time, it's the listening you do that counts. And because your listening time is limited, you'll have to make a quality effort to pick up all the clues you need.

◆ **A receptive, positive state of mind:** run a double check. Write down your goal as soon as you start job hunting and repeat that goal to yourself every day, twenty times a day. Including interview day.

I am in the process of finding the right job for me, it may not be the ideal job first time around, but it's the first step to my perfect career and it will give me the opportunity to develop my skills and meet new challenges.

Listening skills

You may think that talking skills are more appropriate in an interview than listening skills. Wrong. An interview isn't like an exam paper because in interview you have all the answers in front of you. Your interviewer will tell you exactly what they want to hear – if you listen carefully.

Hearing what's not being said. There is so much useful information embedded in the ordinary statements people make. You have probably been using that hidden information to make decisions and relationships for years without realising it. Whenever you rely on your intuition – everybody does, but people who admit to it are often considered flaky – you are actually using this information. The problem is that, if you leave it to your **subconscious**, the facts may get **filtered** through a layer of **prejudices** and **misconceptions** that have built up over the years. If you could access this information directly and analyse it consciously, wouldn't it be more useful?

> 'Concentration is my motto – first honesty, then industry, then concentration.' Andrew Carnegie.

Listening for clues is vital. Whenever your intuition tells you that someone is **uncomfortable**, or **avoiding** a particular issue, or that you've touched upon a hot topic with them, the chances are that your subconscious mind has been noticing some of the following speech patterns.

◆ **Marked out words**. People will often emphasise a particular word over and over again. Once you've *noticed* it, you'll know what's important – or problematical to them. 'Of course, time keeping isn't *everything*'.

◆ **Hesitation** before a question is answered, or asked – this indicates that the topic under discussion is a problem area for the company or the interviewer.

◆ **Digression**. If there's a particular subject (staff turnover for example, or why the previous person left this vacant post) that your interviewer doesn't seem able to stick to without **wandering** off on to something else, there's probably a problem there.

◆ **Failure to respond** to a question or comment. It's surprising how often people **avoid** difficult areas simply by **ignoring** them, and usually in conversation we don't pursue them. It's considered bad form to ask someone the same question twice, just because you didn't get an answer the first time. And you don't want to make your interviewer uncomfortable by harassing them. Fortunately, this works both ways: if you're in a really difficult spot and you're asked for information you don't want to give, you may well get away with ignoring it and giving different information. Of course, this will only work if you are facing an unskilled or inexperienced interviewer.

◆ **Pauses.** These are a lot like marked out words – they always indicate areas of **significance** in the conversation.

◆ **Platitudes.** For example, *'It's the way we do things here'*, or *'We have to be well organised'*, means you have an unskilled interviewer or they aren't really interested in you. Comments like this are not buying signals.

Active listening is very important to both the interviewer and the interviewee. You *can* listen to someone perfectly well when you're leaning back in your chair with your eyes closed. You might miss a few visual cues but they aren't essential – if they were, radio plays and books on tape would be pointless. But the reason that you *don't* lean back and close your eyes in conversation is that it **disconcerts** the other person. The point of active listening is not just to make you hear better, it's to **prompt** the person you're listening to and help them relax.

The chances are that if you're a good communicator, you do these things already. **Awareness** can help you

polish them, but don't just use them like mechanical devices. You'll come across as an alien. Use the following carefully:

◆ Nodding

◆ Interested facial expression

◆ Attentive body language, leaning forward, alert

◆ Repeating key words

◆ Extending questions like *'That's interesting, tell me more'*, *'Why is that important to the company?'*

Use these ideas to help the interviewer become more **expansive**, it saves you having to talk all the time and it **builds rapport**. Showing an interest in what the interviewer says will make him feel good about you and comfortable in your presence. He's much more likely to put you down as an **interested, enthusiastic** candidate.

You can **practise** active listening at home and in the pub – but don't scare the family by suddenly appearing interested in what they say. You might also start to discover things about your nearest and dearest that you'd rather not know.

It's probably safer to spend some time **observing professionals** in action – some TV chat show hosts are brilliant listeners. The best of them are experts at getting other people to talk – sometimes about things they never intended to talk about.

Summary points

◆ Basic sales techniques are the most effective way of buying time to make a good impression in an interview. Recognising the buying signals from an interviewer makes it easy for you to get the timing right.

◆ Asking questions is as important as answering them – you can use them to pace the interview, gain information and put your interviewer into a receptive mode.

◆ Controlling the content of an interview becomes easier if you get used to focusing on your strong points rather than worrying about your negative ones.

◆ Taking notes is another controlling technique which also enables you to monitor your own progress and make sure there are no gaps in your personal presentation.

◆ Listening skills are as relevant for the interviewee as the interviewer – if you pay attention to what the interviewer wants, you will be able to tailor your presentation to suit their requirements.

Chapter 5

Being Remembered for the Right Reasons

'Forget your opponents. Always play against par.' Sam Snead, Golfer

In this Chapter:
- **looking good**
- **feeling good**
- **sounding good**
- **seeing eye to eye**
- **getting into a right state**
- **being interviewed by telephone.**

You won't get the job if you don't leave a **strong, positive visual** and **auditory** impression. But you don't have to be very young and beautiful to get a job – extremely good-looking people are not always taken seriously.

Remember you have a voice. An interview is a **live performance**. Most people ignore their own voices but inflict them on other people. **Tonality** can override content, especially if it's particularly unpleasant. Nobody wants to work within earshot of a dental drill. Even dentists have enough of them eventually.

If you look and sound right, you are well on the way to making your interviewer feel comfortable with you and that means rapport. Also in this chapter we will talk about ways to build rapport with yourself so that you can easily put yourself in the best state to talk yourself into a job.

Telephone interviewing has been added as a reminder that you must work harder to make a good impression over the phone.

Is this you?

◆ Do you feel both confident and comfortable when you go for an interview?

◆ Do you dress in a totally different style to the one you normally use?

◆ Do you look good most of the time or do you make a special effort for outings and interviews?

◆ Are you sometimes so absorbed by how you are feeling and looking that you forget to consider the needs of the person you are communicating with?

- ◆ Would you like to feel better about how you look and how you sound?

- ◆ Do you think increased personal confidence would help you build faster rapport?

Looking good

Once, during a tube strike in Central London, a female applicant for a senior PA role cycled to her interview. She arrived in leggings, trainers and a helmet, rather than a suit and high heels. Her logic was that the other applicants would postpone the interview until public transport was available and that she would get points for energy and initiative. It didn't work that way because the man she was going to work for was a stickler for appearances. Knowing that this was a woman who would turn up to work on time, come what may, could not erase from his mind her unsuitable appearance and a later applicant was given the job. However, a prospective employer with a less conservative outlook might have made a different decision.

The lesson here is that there's more to looking good than meets the eye of the applicant. You need to know what looks good to your prospective employer and the **importance of appearance** in general to a particular company. This, once again, requires that you do your homework.

'Polish yourself up first and your act second. Otherwise you won't have an act.' Georgie Bennett.

IBM ran a study to find out whether managers were affected by what their colleagues and employees were wearing. The results were remarkable. Men and women wearing **dark blue suits** with **white shirts** and **black shoes** were considered 40% more **believable** than anyone else. Next came those wearing dark grey, followed by those in light grey. Bottom of the credibility ratings were the people who turned up in camel-coloured suits, brown shoes and multicoloured shirts.

The chances are that these attitudes to dress are still pretty much universal in large companies. So how do you match the interviewer's expectations while not looking so grey and anonymous that you are immediately forgotten? **Wear one striking item** – it could be a tie for a man, or a scarf or brooch for a woman. Not something offensive, but something **memorable**. Obviously if you're applying for work in the media, or farming, different dress codes may apply (though not necessarily for the interview).

The most important rule of appropriate appearance is to concentrate on looking **clean** and **smart** rather than glamorous – unless you are applying for a theatrical or modelling position.

Make sure you are:

◆ **Clean** – shower and wear clean clothes and shoes, minimise perfume and aftershave.

◆ **Covered** – always wear a jacket and tights with your skirt or socks with your trousers, the only visible bare flesh should be your face, neck and hands.

◆ **Checked** – for smudges and dandruff: take a hairbrush, mirror, tissues and sticky tape.

◆ **Creaseless** – don't wear linen.

Feeling good

Your first task as an interviewee is to make the interviewer feel good. You can use the **mirroring** and **pacing** techniques we talked about in earlier chapters, and tuning in to language patterns. But there's more. Put yourself in the interviewer's shoes. How do they feel? What are they looking for? That's the start of rapport.

It will help if you take out the tension. You want the interviewer to respect you and take you seriously – they will be more comfortable with this than if you grovel. Unless of course they are on a power trip of their own, in which case you don't want to work for them. There's a big **difference** between **aggression** and **assertiveness** and you need to be clear about which is which and what you usually do.

This is where your group interview practice will come in handy and here are some exercises you can use to help you prepare for potentially difficult situations:

Smiling convincingly is hard to do to order. Most people don't smile enough and many people have fallen into a habitual social smile that would do equally well as a grimace. It certainly doesn't convey pleasure.

So, practise. It's useful in any *meet and greet* situation. People who smile convincingly when they don't necessarily feel great are the ones who get **better service** in shops and restaurants and attract all the attention at parties. It's almost impossible to be angry with someone who stands tall and walks towards you, hand outstretched, making eye contact. In your practice interviews, run through some role-play scenarios where one of you tries to maintain an aggressive stance in the face of their partner who walks towards them grinning cheerfully and expectantly.

A **double bind** is a complex psychological concept – somebody is giving you two (or more) conflicting messages at the same time. But you can practise getting out of the minor versions that are likely to occur in interview and stop yourself inflicting them on other people. It's very demotivating when you're all set up to make a great impression and you're met by a jaded interviewer who tells you your CV looks impressive in a completely disinterested voice. You can deal with situations like this much more effectively if you play with the mechanics of them and learn how to turn them around.

'Charm is the quality in others that makes us more satisfied with ourselves.' Henri Frederic Amiel.

In your interview practice group, sit with a partner facing you. Ask a third person to give you a discussion topic and time you for three one-minute sessions.

Session one: **Agree verbally**, but **disagree** radically with your body language. Break eye contact, lean back, look away, fidget with something…

Session two: **Mirror** your partner's **body language** as closely as you can while **disagreeing verbally** with everything he says.

Session three: Repeat session one, but this time, one of you continues to **agree verbally** while **disagreeing** with **body language**, while the other attempts to **regain rapport** by using very **positive body language** – smiling, leaning forward, eye contact etc.

You will have realised that the verbal message is less powerful than the body language.

Contrived and exaggerated as this whole exercise may be, I've never met anyone who didn't gain something useful from it. It illustrates the **power** and **simplicity** of body language compared to verbal content because:

◆ It is difficult to be verbally aggressive or even disinterested with someone who is being physically positive and conciliatory.

◆ You can practise **pacing** and **leading**, raising an interviewer's level of interest and involvement, increasing the energy level in an interview and gaining commitment.

◆ Check out your own natural body language tendencies and learn to **moderate** or **exaggerate** them at will. You will get feedback both from your partner and the referee and also from yourself – you will quickly know which behaviour is more difficult for you and which comes naturally.

Agreeing with disagreeable people can work to your advantage. If you know that you've a tendency to be aggressive when you're nervous, there are some techniques you can use to make sure that you are relaxed. But, if you still find yourself in an interview situation where stress – or an aggressive interviewer – is winding you up like a spring there are two things you can do:

◆ **Breath deeply and slowly**; this always has a calming effect and it's difficult to be loud and aggressive when your whole body is relaxed.

◆ Imagine your interviewer as a **cartoon character**, or just give them a Mickey Mouse voice. Only use this one if you find someone seriously threatening – in borderline cases it may make you giggle.

Sounding good

Listen to yourself. Do you remember music and sounds more easily than pictures? If you do, then your preferred representational system is probably **auditory** (Chapter 3). Auditory people tend to have low pitched, pleasant speaking voices because they listen to themselves. But most of us have a visual bias and wouldn't necessarily recognise our own voice on a recording.

Have you ever heard yourself speaking on tape? If not, now is the time. Listen critically. Ask other people for feedback.

> 'If I'm selling a BMW that sounds like a Lada, I leave the test drive 'til the last minute.' Murray Ricardo, Brecknock Motors.

If in doubt, **lower your voice** a tone or two. This takes practice. But it's less stressful for you and more pleasant for other people. If you find it difficult, lower your breathing as well, take your breaths from your **abdomen**, rather than your upper chest – this calms the mind as well as improving the tonality of your voice.

Do you have a strong **regional accent**? That's all right, as long as it's Scottish or Welsh and not too strong. Sadly, whether we like it or not, most other pronounced regional accents meet with disapproval from people who don't have them. Most people know this and auditory people have an easy solution. They **tune in** so quickly to other people's speech patterns that after ten minutes conversation, they have acquired it themselves. This is like mirroring, it only works if it comes naturally. If your interviewer suspects that you are mimicking their Liverpool or South London dialect you will find the interview terminates fast.

Seeing eye to eye

Eye contact is difficult for many people. They know they have to do it but they don't like it, so they either hold the gaze for too long and make the interviewer uncomfortable, or they don't hold it long enough and make themselves look shifty. People who make good eye contact take their cue from the person they are looking at. They look down when the first sign of discomfort appears.

'Remember, when you smile, the mouth comes in last.' Mischa Gold. The Eyes Have It.

If you suspect that eye contact is a problem for you there are three things you can do about it:

◆ **Practise** with your Interview Group and get some accurate feedback.

◆ In the interview, make sure you have a cup of coffee and your CV to look down at from time to time.

◆ Don't look directly at the other person's eyes. **Focusing** on their **nose** or **forehead** will feel more comfortable.

The sincerity triangle runs between the eyes and down to the nose. Avoid the triangle which includes the nose and the mouth – it's inappropriate for a business interview. Never allow your gaze to wander lower than your interviewer's face.

Getting into a right state

Putting the interviewer into a receptive state is going to be much easier – in fact it will come naturally – if you first pay attention to your own frame of mind. Having a killer CV and all the answers isn't going to help if you're vibrating with tension when you walk into the room.

Breathing, fortunately, isn't an activity which requires conscious thought. But when you're stressed your body prepares for action. And if the stress is caused by a situation that requires supreme calm rather than a physical response, this works against you. Learning to **control** your own **breathing** is the answer.

'The height of your accomplishments will equal the depth of your convictions.' William Scolavino.

If you **meditate** or practise **yoga**, you'll already be familiar with this idea, but, if you've never thought about it before, breathing control is one of the easiest and most effective techniques for clearing the mind and steadying the hand. If you've never tried it, don't wait until you get to the interview. Start practising now.

Sitting or standing, **focus** on a point three fingers below your navel and breath in deeply through your nose, taking your breath right down to that point. Hold the breath for three seconds and slowly let it go. **Be aware** of that breath all the way **in** and all the way **out**. Repeat this two or three times while you sit in the waiting room and notice how much steadier you seem to be and how much taller you feel when you stand up to meet your interviewer.

Being interviewed by telephone

Most of the advice on face-to-face interviews also applies to contact with a potential employer over the telephone.

'Nothing is so contagious as enthusiasm; it moves stones, it charms brutes. Enthusiasm is the genius of sincerity and truth accomplishes no victories without it.' Edward G E Bulwer-Lytton.

Every contact you have with a prospective employer, however brief and indirect, **is an interview**. Calling to make an appointment or check an address gives you long enough to make an impression over the phone. The advantage with phone calls is that you don't have to worry about the suit and the dandruff. On the other hand, you are missing out on visual cues and the interviewer isn't getting the benefit of your smile.

◆ You can still make the interviewer feel good about you by **mirroring** their **verbal patterns**, and using a **low-pitched, pleasant** tone of **voice**. Your voice is vitally important when it's the only point of contact you have.

◆ Eye contact may be impossible, but you should still **look** at the **phone** – if you're looking at something else, you are not giving the conversation your full energy and attention and that will show.

◆ Don't give up on the body language either – it's different in a phone call, but still important. It's better to **stand** than **sit**, your voice will sound more energetic. And smile, of course. **You can hear a smile** – it affects the way the words come out.

◆ You can't know when you'll get the important call, so, when you're job hunting, make an effort to **answer** the phone **clearly** and **pleasantly**, with *'Hello'* and the number. Make sure that unreliable family members are not likely to pick it up and answer it for you.

◆ **Use active listening**. Say *'Mmm'* and *'Yes'* and ask questions regularly so that the other person knows you are paying attention.

◆ **Take notes** while you're on the phone – then you can quickly re-cap for the other person if they are called away.

Summary points

◆ **Looking good is important. When the interviewer reviews the applications, visual images will come to their mind first.**

◆ **Feeling good is the second thing the interviewer will remember about you. They will remember whether they felt comfortable with you.**

◆ **Sounding good gives you an instant advantage over the 60% of applicants who neglect their voices.**

◆ **Seeing eye to eye for the right length of time and intensity is surprisingly easy to get wrong but fortunately easy to put right. It's back to the Practice Group if you need help with this one.**

◆ **Getting into a right state by controlling your own breathing can be the key to staying in control of the interview.**

◆ **Any contact you have with your prospective employer by phone is a job interview so take phone calls seriously.**

Chapter 6

Standard Interview Questions

'The will to win is not nearly as important as the will to prepare to win.'

In this Chapter:

◆ **your questions answered**

◆ **criteria questions**

◆ **knowing how to handle questions**

◆ **avoiding traps for the unwary**

◆ **observing the golden rule**

◆ **handling tough interview questions**

◆ **if you do nothing else...**

I was interviewing someone recently and, when I asked him to tell me which aspect of his work he enjoyed the least, he said *'Oh, I never know what to say to that one.'* *'Well, why don't you think of some answers in advance?'* I asked. *'I don't know,'* he said. *'It seems a bit like cheating. Anyway, I'm always so relieved when an interview is over that I don't think about questions until the next one's on top of me.'*

Talk to people who already work for your target company. Find out what kind of situations arise and what is important in management terms. Get together with your Practice Group and ask each other difficult interview questions.

You won't necessarily have direct experience of every work scenario that is raised in an interview. The important thing is to know what *should* happen in the most likely situations.

Is this you?

◆ Do you think of the right answers to questions about half an hour after the interview has finished?

◆ Have you ever said to yourself, or a friend: 'I hate that question – I never know what to say.'?

◆ Have you ever been completely blank in interview when you've been asked to describe a particular situation, only to recall the perfect illustration in the traffic jam on the way home?

Your questions answered

There are general rules for specific questions:

◆ **Listen carefully** – make sure you're answering the question that's been asked.

◆ **Stick** to **providing** what's been **requested**, don't give superfluous information – it confuses the situation and won't do you any good.

◆ **Don't interrupt** the interviewer when you think you know what they're going to ask. Wait until you've got the whole story.

◆ Don't flood the interviewer with information when they say *'Tell me about yourself'*. Prepare a statement which is relevant to the particular vacancy and try it out on your Practice Group first.

Criteria questions

When you've done your homework on the position you're applying for and you know what selection criteria they are using, you can prepare in advance some examples which show that you are the right person for the job.

Likely criteria are:

◆ Initiative

◆ Stress tolerance

- ◆ Adaptability
- ◆ Leadership
- ◆ Problem analysis
- ◆ Interpersonal skills
- ◆ Team attitude
- ◆ Reliability
- ◆ Persuasiveness
- ◆ Innovation
- ◆ Delegation
- ◆ Diligence.

There are many others – it all depends on the type of vacancy. No matter what your profession, you are likely to be asked a question about how you shape up in at least one of these areas. The phrasing of the questions depends on the interviewer's skill. An inexperienced interviewer is likely to ask leading questions:

Q 'Would you describe yourself as a well-organised person?'

A 'Yes.'

This is a hopeless question and an unhelpful answer. A more skilful interviewer might ask:

Q 'How do you plan your day?'

A 'I review the day before I go to sleep at night and make some final notes in my diary about anything that's left over. Then, in the morning, I'm always on the early train, so I go through my detailed list. I prioritise my tasks and estimate how long each one is likely to take – allowing some leeway for emergencies. The last thing I do before I go home at night is review what's been done and what hasn't.'

Always give **specific, detailed answers**. No matter how inadequate the question, the interviewer will still be dissatisfied with inadequate answers. If they don't get enough information to make a decision about you, it won't matter whether it's your fault or theirs, you still won't be selected. Do yourself a favour by giving comprehensive answers.

Knowing how to handle questions

Answering a question with a statement
This is a useful technique for questions that don't have a 'right' answer.

Q 'Do you often find yourself working late?'

Normal behaviour in one company might be **poor** time management in another. Respond with another question:

A 'What's typical in your department? I like to be efficient but I'm willing to be flexible.'

Don't answer questions that show you in a **bad light**.

When politicians are asked difficult questions they give statements instead of answers. You don't want to admit how many times you had flu last winter or that you are waiting to hear from five other interviews.

Q 'How is your health? Do you often take sick days?'

Q 'Are you being interviewed for any other jobs?'

Confident remarks about the importance of a healthy lifestyle or the fact that your job search is in the early stages are a diplomatic option here.

If you respond promptly and confidently to a question, what you say will usually be accepted as an answer – even if it isn't.

Asking for the answer

Q 'Do you think you have the right experience for this post?'

It's easy to get this wrong – either too much or too little experience could rule you out of the job. **Find out more** about what they want before committing yourself – if you have too little experience, think of some areas in which you have done similar work.

A 'Perhaps you can tell me a bit more about exactly what you're looking for. Do you need someone who has specialised in telesales?'

Changing the question

Q 'What kind of things do you worry about?'

In questions like this, you can **defuse** the question by taking out the loaded word when you answer.

A 'I think worrying is pretty pointless – I prefer to take action and make changes. However, the areas that do **concern** me are meeting deadlines, reducing staff turnover, reaching sales targets and getting the best out of my team.'

Avoiding traps for the unwary

Beware of 'either/or' questions. They are usually traps for the unwary.

Q 'What is most important in the workplace, total honesty, or supportiveness towards colleagues?'

This appears to be straightforward on the face of it. After all, both honesty and supportiveness to colleagues are important. On closer examination however, the interviewer is asking you to choose between loyalty to the company and loyalty to your workmates.

A 'I think that honesty and supportiveness are both important. But obviously I couldn't support a colleague who was behaving dishonestly either toward the company or with a client.'

That would depend on is one of the most useful phrases in interview and can be used as a last resort.

Q 'What would you do if you felt your line manager was dishonest/incompetent/had a personal problem?'

A 'That would depend on the seriousness of the problem and whether or not it was affecting his ability to do his job. Obviously in the case of dishonesty or incompetence, action would be required. A personal problem might or might not affect others in the workplace and I would need to make a judgement on that.'

Observing the golden rule

The Golden Rule of answering interview questions is **always to give a positive answer**. It doesn't matter if your last employer was an alcoholic pervert who was fiddling the books and blaming you for it – your reasons for moving on are always forward-looking and pro-active.

Q 'What did you like/dislike about your last job?'

Treat this question as an opportunity to make it clear that you are a positive, forward-looking person. In interview, you should say that you liked everything about your last job, but pick out something with the new job that is different and challenging. Don't fall into the trap of saying what you want the new job to give you – emphasise what you have to offer and use the word **contribution**.

A 'I enjoyed my last job and gained some useful sales experience, but I am looking for an opportunity to contribute that to building a new team with a higher conversion rate.'

People are tainted by their misfortunes. You will attract not sympathy but distrust if you appear to have walked out of a hotbed of dissent and corruption and a prospective employer will suspect that you have brought with you some traces of the problems you are claiming to have left behind.

Typical questions that might tempt you to be negative include:

Q 'What did you think of your last boss?'

Q 'What is the most difficult situation you have faced at work?'

Never say anything detrimental about your colleagues, managers or the system.

You should always sell the benefit, not the product. Find a hook in the question to make a strong point about your particular suitability for the job.

Q 'Why do you want this job?'

Q 'Why should we offer you this job?'

Q 'What are the reasons for your success?'

Q 'Give an example of yourself as a team player who can also work alone.'

Q 'What are you best at?'

Q 'What are your greatest achievements?'

Q 'What have you learned in your time with...?'

When asked what you're good at, **make sure it's something they want**. It's no good making a virtue out of being prepared to start early if the company deals largely with the US and wants staff who are prepared to work late.

And what if you're asked to talk about your personal downside – as you almost certainly will be. How can you remain positive when your interviewer wants you to tell tales on yourself? It's no good pretending you're perfect because that throws doubt on all the other claims you've made.

Q 'What area of work do you feel least confident with?'

Q 'What do your colleagues see as your greatest weakness?'

Offer imperfections that come from inexperience or something that might be a virtue in another setting.

A 'I would like some more training/experience with appraisal interviewing – my staff seem happy enough but I would welcome the chance to raise my skill level in that area.'

Handling tough interview questions

We've already covered the classic questions. Most people know how to answer questions about their weak points and come up with convincing reasons for wanting a particular job. But it's the apparently innocuous or totally unexpected questions that often trip even the more experienced interviewees.

Rules to remember

◆ Innocent or irrelevant questions are traps for the unwary and opportunities for candidates who are on the ball.

◆ Always be on the lookout for a question or comment that might be a hook for some positive information about you and the job you're discussing.

◆ Answers should always end with a positive comment, giving the impression that you are a positive person.

♦ Watch out for ways of tuning the answer to the requirements of the job. The interview is primarily about the job, not about you.

♦ Avoid going into detail about anything that isn't job related. Offer summaries.

Double edged swords

Q 'What did you think about... in the news this morning?'
♦ **Don't** wade straight in with an opinion unless you're absolutely sure what the company standpoint will be. If it's an issue that's critical to your personal belief and the company you're applying to has a different standpoint, you may need to think twice about whether you really want the job.

♦ **Do** agree that it's controversial and, if you think it's relevant, ask the interviewer what they think the impact might be. Open up the discussion before you venture an opinion.

Q 'What is your overall impression of us?'
♦ **Don't** say 'I think this is a fabulous company and I can't wait to work here,' and don't go to the other extreme and start criticising the office furniture.

♦ **Do** say you like the mission, style and values, commenting individually on each: 'I really like what you're doing/selling and the high tech/relaxed/ customer focused environment...'

Q 'What will you do if you don't get this job?'

◆ **Don't** say you won't care, but on the other hand you won't be devastated either.

◆ **Do** stay cool and professional. It will be a disappointment because you've enjoyed the interview and you think you have a lot to offer in the role, you are eager to work for such an exciting/fast growing/ high profile company. But you are looking for the right job and you're prepared to put in the necessary time to find it.

Q 'Do you think the interview is going well?'

◆ **Don't** say 'I'm not very good at interviews' but, on the other hand don't say you think it's going well if it clearly isn't.

◆ **Do** start with a compliment to the interviewer: 'You've asked me some pretty searching questions and I hope I've given you the information you're looking for. I feel that my skills and experience are well suited to this position but are there any areas you'd still like to ask me about?' Turn the question around as fast as you can and ask the interviewer what they think. This is a useful feedback opportunity.

Q 'Do you think you've lived up to your potential?'

◆ **Don't** be defensive, this question is not meant to make you feel that you haven't lived up to your potential and it's more about seeing how you react when challenged than anything else.

◆ **Do** come up with some positive examples of how you feel you have lived up to your potential and conclude by saying that you still have some professional goals that you are striving for. If your progress has been slower than the interviewer might have expected you can say something like 'I wanted to make sure that I was building my career on a solid skill base.'

Q 'What sort of questions intimidate you?'

◆ **Don't** say there aren't any, that sounds arrogant.

◆ **Do** choose a question you've already been asked. This flatters the interviewer, making them feel extremely perceptive, insightful and in control.

Apparently banal but potentially lethal questions

Q 'Did you have a hard time finding us?'

◆ **Don't** admit it if you did. It makes you look stupid and implies their directions weren't so good either. It won't get you any sympathy – *especially* if you were late.

◆ **Do** compliment their directions, or, if you can, turn it to a job advantage by bringing in some extra information – 'I went to college around here' or 'I travel this route to my evening class ...'. Don't make something up, but if you can slip in something useful, go for it.

Q 'How was your journey?'

◆ **Don't** go into a lot of detail. If the trains were late don't make a big deal out of it.

◆ **Do** make a positive statement regardless of what the journey was actually like. Negative statements make you seem like a negative person. And, if you can, add something that makes you look industrious and highlights a skill: 'I got a seat so I could catch up on some reading, which was useful.'

Q 'You look tanned – have you been on holiday?'
◆ **Don't** launch into a long description of your latest exotic holiday or your sessions at the tanning salon. It may give the impression that your priorities aren't work related.

◆ **Do** say something like 'I enjoy being outdoors when I'm not at work.'

Questions that are so straightforward they may fool you into not making enough effort to answer

Q 'What do you prefer to be called?'
◆ **Don't** tell the story of how you came to be nicknamed Bubbles.

◆ **Do** say you are happy to be addressed by your first name (given in full) and then ask what the company policy is about names – formal or informal.

Q 'I see you're reading *The Economist*, what did you think of that article about . . .?'
◆ **Don't** say 'I haven't got to that one yet,' or pretend you have and waffle.

◆ **Do** make sure that if you walk into an interview with a serious publication under your arm that you've read and understood it all, even if it's not something you'd normally read.

Q 'We have a pretty good cricket team here, do you play?'
◆ **Don't** say you do play if you don't and don't say you can't stand the game either.

◆ **Do** make a positive comment like, 'I don't understand the finer points, but I like to watch on a warm summer evening – what league do you compete in?'

Open-ended quicksand questions

This is where the interviewer hands you the rope and waits to see how long it's going to take you to hang yourself.

Q 'Tell me about yourself.'
◆ **Don't** even attempt a summary. The only things about you that matter in this situation are the job related ones.

◆ **Do** pick out a couple of things about you which are also particularly relevant to this particular job. You can think this through as part of your interview preparation.

Q 'What are your priorities?'
◆ **Don't** talk about family or spiritual quests. This, like every other question is about work.

◆ **Do** talk in general about meeting targets, being well organised and focused. Add specific priorities that are relevant to this particular position.

Questions that tell you not to bother

Q 'Have you ever lodged a complaint about sexual harassment?'

Questions like this are generally markers that indicate there may be a problem within this organisation.

Q 'What would you do if your child was sick and you had tight deadlines to meet at work?'

An experienced interviewer will know they shouldn't put you on the spot like this. In some cases it's a way of finding out whether or not you have dependent children.

Q 'Are you planning to start a family?'

They aren't allowed to ask you this but if you refuse to answer it will be taken as a yes.

Q 'Are you married or in a long-term relationship?'

Again, this is a question you don't have to answer, but whatever you say might get you into trouble, depending on the personal views of the interviewer.

Q 'That's an interesting accent/unusual surname, where are you from? Were you born here? What language do you speak at home?'

Of course, this may be simple curiosity, but it's more likely to be an indication that the interviewer is concerned about ethnicity and may have some underlying prejudices.

If you do nothing else ...

If you do nothing else that I've suggested in this book, at the very least you **must arm** yourself with the answers to the following questions. This is not a one-off exercise; take the time to run through your answers before each interview, tweaking them appropriately.

For example – here are the replies you might give if you were going for the zoo keeper's job:

Q 'Why did you leave your last job?'

A 'Because I wanted to get out of an office environment and use my knowledge about animals and my customer interface experience.'

You might think there was only one answer to this. But, unless you were fired, there's a different answer for every job application you make. The only good reason for leaving a job as far as an employer is concerned is that the job they are offering is a better one. Nobody wants to employ somebody who is likely to walk out just because they are bored or unfulfilled.

Q 'What is your greatest failing?'

A 'I sometimes get impatient with paperwork and I know that I work better in a hands on environment.'

You can't get away with saying you haven't got any failings – but you can always come up with something that may have been a failing in your last job but would be a positive advantage in the new one.

Q 'How do you think your colleagues would describe you?'

A 'At the last 360-degree appraisal I was described by most people as being demanding to work with but a good team player.'

This question has two built-in traps:

◆ self deprecation
◆ self aggrandisement

The way around the situation is to come up with a **real** answer – in writing if possible. If written appraisals are not built in to your current employment, you could organise a 'testimonial'.

Q 'What annoys you most?'

A 'Not reaching my targets for the day because I've forgotten to plan something in. I can cope with emergencies – there's nothing you can do to predict those.'

Again, try to pick something that is a strong positive point in the job you are applying for. Never choose anything to do with colleagues or management – warning bells ring for prospective employers if they think you are likely to find fault with co-workers.

Always choose something to do with an external system or a fairly harmless failing of your own.

Q 'Why are you the best candidate for this job?'

A 'Because I have a lot of experience with wild animals and I am passionate about communicating my enthusiasm to other people.'

Be strong and positive about this and pick two criteria.

Now run through this exercise again with a different job in mind. Instead of zoo keeping, suppose you decided to use your biology A level and your PR background to go into veterinary nursing instead?

Q 'Why did you leave your last job?'

A 'Because I wanted to study animal care in more depth and also spend more time with 'real' people and everyday issues.'

There are as many reasons for leaving a job as there are new jobs to go for. The 'wrong' answer here would have been because you were fed up with the shallow world of advertising. Interviewers are wary of people who see a new job as an escape from dissatisfaction or, worse still, as a route to discovering the meaning of life. These are only acceptable reasons if you are applying for a voluntary post in a charitable organisation.

Q 'What is your greatest failing?'

A 'I always want to follow through with a problem and find out what is really happening.'

This might be considered pernickety in the world of PR. But it has to be useful when a young mother comes in with a dog that is constantly being sick. Just what are the children feeding it?

Q 'How do you think your colleagues would describe you?'

A 'At the last 360 degree appraisal I was described as pleasant and hard working – but what they wanted was dynamic and ruthless!'

A fault in one setting can be a virtue in another.

Q 'What annoys you most?'

A 'Days when I'm on the phone all the time rearranging meetings and lunch appointments, but nothing actually gets done.'

Of course, questions like this are easier when you are going for radically different jobs to the one you currently have. There's less likely to be overlap in what annoys you.

But when you're stuck, there are still a few universally annoying things (like this one).

Q 'Why are you the best candidate for this job?'

A 'Because I am very good with people and I love animals, plus I want to work locally – I'm fed up with commuting.'

Again, relatively easy if you stick to the criteria.

There's no harm in having a personal reason – like not wanting to commute any more – it's more likely to make you contented with the new job.

Summary points

◆ **Your questions answered – one of the most common complaints about interviews is that people can never think of good answers until it's too late. There's a simple solution to this – preparation and practice.**

◆ **Criteria questions are particularly easy to prepare for – provided you have taken the trouble to find out what the criteria are, you can methodically set up the answers you need on paper or on your PC.**

◆ Answering a question with a question is a technique best practised live. Get your practice group to fire some difficult ones at you so that you can get into the habit of thinking on your feet.

◆ Using a difficult question to make a positive statement is a political skill that you can see in action on television whenever there is a news item. Learn from the professionals.

◆ Asking for the answer is the only way to get some questions right.

◆ Changing the question is fine if it's not one that you want to answer.

◆ Traps for the unwary include either/or questions and can often be sidestepped with techniques like *that depends. . .*

◆ The golden rule is, of course, **be positive**.

◆ If you do nothing else, prepare a selection of answers to the questions we've listed, discuss them, think about them and practise them. Then, step into your interview with confidence.

If you want to know how...

◆ To buy a home in the sun, and let it out

◆ To move overseas, and work well with the people who live there

◆ To get the job you want, in the career you like

◆ To plan a wedding, and make the Best Man's speech

◆ To build your own home, or manage a conversion

◆ To buy and sell houses, and make money from doing so

◆ To gain new skills and learning, at a later time in life

◆ To empower yourself, and improve your lifestyle

◆ To start your own business, and run it profitably

◆ To prepare for your retirement, and generate a pension

◆ To improve your English, or write a PhD

◆ To be a more effective manager, and a good communicator

◆ To write a book, and get it published

If you want to know how to do all these things and much, much more...

howtobooks

If you want to know how...to change your career for the better

"We owe it to ourselves and to our families to find rewarding careers as part of a balanced life. A successful career move involves people matching their ideas, passions and goals to the needs of employers and vice versa. People need jobs and jobs need people. This book is to help people take a new look at themselves and supply them with the tools they need to make their career move – to a place where they can satisfy most of their needs and some of their wants. Whatever move you want to make it has to start from a basis of self-knowledge. An understanding of your needs and wants, and knowledge of what you can contribute.

There is a secret to successful job search. It is persistence. Seek and you shall find."

Graham Green

The Career Change Handbook
Find out what you're good at and enjoy; and get someone to pay you for it. It's as simple and as difficult as that.
Graham Green

"Interesting and to the point advice." – *The Guardian*

"There is little of the silly and trivial advice often found in career advice books. – *The Career Change Handbook* gives incisive advice." *Tyrone Times*

ISBN 1 85703 865 7

If you want to know how...to prepare for interviews

"It's the interviewer's prerogative to throw just about any question they can think of at the interviewee. So you might think that it's almost impossible to prepare for an interview. But the truth is that 80% of interview questions revolve around 20 common themes. And many interviewees let themselves down by not thinking about these themes, preparing and rehearsing responses to them.

Many candidates then go on to create a wrong impression. Remember that an interviewer has to *like* you and warm to you as a person as well as want to work with you because you answer the questions well. I see too many candidates who talk too much or come across as nervous or unfriendly. If you get the chance to rehearse with a friend and get some feedback on just how you come across, you will improve your chances no end."

Rob Yeung

Successful Interviews Every Time
Rob Yeung

"*Successful Interviews* is the type of book that one may not wish to share with others who are job seeking in competition with oneself. Nevertheless, I owe a debt of gratitude to Dr Rob Yeung for sharing his experiences with us..." – *S. Lewis, Coventry*

"This book is an invaluable source of information for job hunters on preparing for interviews, tests and assessment centres." – *Jonathan Turpin, Chief Executive of job hunting website fish4jobs.co.uk*

ISBN 1 85703 978 5

If you want to know how...to successfully apply for a job

"Being successful in a fiercely competitive jobs market takes time and effort. Spurring a recruiter into wanting to know more about you is the secret of success with any application. Each one must be special: it has to say – 'Here I am. This is what I can offer you.' This book is designed to help you present your skills in a practical and marketable manner and ultimately achieve your goal. How you approach this crucial first stage is vitally important, only successful applications lead to interviews."

Judith Johnstone

The Job Application Handbook
A systematic guide to applying for a job
Judith Johnstone

Whether you're leaving university, re-entering the job market, facing redundancy or simply wanting a change, this handbook reveals the best ways to approach potential employers.

ISBN 1 85703 992 0

If you want to know how...to write a winning CV

"Employers want to see what you can offer; they want to see it presented quickly and simply. And they want to see it in a format that is good for them to process through their recruitment procedures. A little research can not only make a CV look good, but can also make it pass quickly to the right person, getting you the opportunity to interview and make a personal impression, showing employers why they should hire you, and allowing you to decide whether you really do want to work for them."

Julie-Ann Amos

Write a Winning CV
Essential CV writing skills that will get you the job you want
Julie-Ann Amos

"If you are in the market for advice, *Write A Winning CV* is a great starting point." – *The Guardian*

"There is no shortage of publications concerning CVs and covering letters; so what has this new contender got to offer? Quite a lot, as it turns out. For a start it is written not by a careers adviser, but by a recruitment specialist...it is up-to-date, written with authority and packed full of helpful advice." – *N. Evans, Occupational Psychologist, Newscheck*

ISBN 1 85703 840 1

How To Books are available through all good bookshops, or you can order direct from us through Grantham Book Services.

Tel: +44 (0)1476 541080
Fax: +44 (0)1476 541061
Email: orders@gbs.tbs-ltd.co.uk

Or via our website

www.howtobooks.co.uk

To order via any of these methods please quote the title(s) of the book(s) and your credit card number together with its expiry date.

For further information about our books and catalogue, please contact:

How To Books
3 Newtec Place
Magdalen Road
Oxford OX4 1RE

Visit our website at

www.howtobooks.co.uk

Or you can contact us by email at
info@howtobooks.co.uk